\,nev-ər-t͟hə-ˈless\ *adv* : a bridge between two opposing id
ˈless\ *adv* : a bridge between two opposing ideas or sets of
s \,nev-ər-t͟hə-ˈless\ *adv* : a bridge between two opposing i
ev-ər-t͟hə-ˈless\ *adv* : a bridge between two opposing ideas
ll ne·ver·the·less \,nev-ər-t͟hə-less\ *adv* : in spite of that : F
·the·less \,nev-ər-t͟hə-ˈless\ *adv* : a bridge between two op

NEVERTHELESS

r-t͟hə-ˈless\ *adv* : a bridge between two opposing ideas or
he·less \,nev-ər-t͟hə-ˈless\ *adv* :a bridge between two oppo
ess \,nev-ər-t͟hə-ˈless\ *adv* : a bridge between two opposing
facts ll ne·ver·the·less \,nev-ər-t͟hə-less \ *adv* : a bridge be
·the·less \,nev-ər-t͟hə-ˈless\ *adv* : a bridge between two op
ɪev-ər-t͟hə-ˈless\ *adv* : a bridge between two opposing idea
ə·less \,nev-ər-t͟hə-less\ *adv* : a bridge between two oppos
r-t͟hə-ˈless\ *adv* : a bridge between two opposing ideas or s

MARK RUTLAND

he·less \,nev-ər-t͟hə-ˈless\ dge between two oppo
ss \,nev-ər-t͟hə-ˈless\ ween two opposing
facts ll ne·ver·the·less \,nev-ər-t͟hə-less \ *adv* : in spite of t.
ə·less \,nev-ər-t͟hə-less\ *adv* : a bridge between two oppos
-ər-t͟hə-ˈless\ *adv* : a bridge between two opposing ideas or
ss \,nev-ər-t͟hə-ˈless\ *adv* : a bridge between two opposing
ɪə-ˈless\ *adv* : a bridge between two opposing ideas or sets
ess \,nev-ər-t͟hə-ˈless\ *adv* : a bridge between two opposin
\,nev-ər-t͟hə-ˈless\ *adv* : a bridge between two opposing ide
:ts ll ne·ver·the·less \,nev-ər-t͟hə-less \ *adv* : a bridge betwe
ss \,nev-ər-t͟hə-ˈless\ *adv* e between two opposing

Charisma
HOUSE
Books about Spirit-Led Living

t͟hə-ˈless\ *adv* : a bridge b wo opposing ideas or se
,nev-ər-t͟hə-ˈless\ *adv* : a bridge between two opposing ide
ess\ *adv* : a bridge between two opposing ideas or sets of
\,nev-ər-t͟hə-ˈless\ *adv* : a bridge between two opposing ic

NEVERTHELESS by Mark Rutland
Published by Charisma House
A part of Strang Communications Company
600 Rinehart Road
Lake Mary, Florida 32746
www.charismahouse.com

Author's note: All Scripture references, unless otherwise indicated, are from the King James Version. This is not because I am devoted to the King James Version's authenticity, but because of its beautiful use of the very word about which this book is written.

Cover design by Rachel Campbell
Interior design by Debbie Lewis

Library of Congress Catalog Card Number: 2001096340
International Standard Book Number: 0-88419-847-2

02 03 04 05   8 7 6 5 4 3
Printed in the United States of America

For Samuel Odarno—
my brother, friend and
comrade in arms

ACKNOWLEDGMENTS

For tireless work on this manuscript and on many such projects for which they receive altogether too little praise, thanks or reward, I wish to acknowledge several people.

The editorial oversight and project direction of my wife, Alison, were invaluable. Dr. Gordon Miller also lent his considerable abilities to the editorial task, made all the greater by this author. Mrs. Glenna Rakes, my secretary, was the chief typist, encourager and den mother. My own mother, Rosemary Rutland, served as the line editor and applied the creative spurs gently and well.

The entire project was conceived and more or less commanded by my son, Travis, the media director at Global Servants, Inc. I cannot, for the life of me, remember when he became my boss. Still, I take satisfaction in knowing that I met the deadline even if it was set by a benevolent dictator in his mid-twenties.

To all, named and unnamed, who have contributed, I say thank you.

—MARK RUTLAND

Contents

INTRODUCTION

OVER THE THRESHOLD

For one wild, terrible, wonderful and quite unforgettable season, I coached an inner-city football team. I actually fancied, in that quixotic moment, that they were learning something from me. I imagined that indelible life lessons were being imparted by their painfully youthful coach—profitable and important lessons that would become a deep-tissue part of them for the rest of their lives.

Now, much, much older and slightly more educated by life, I know the truth of it to be a two-edged sword. Today I am quite certain that few of those players, now middle-aged men, can even remember me, and absolutely none recall my name. I also doubt that I made much of a lasting impression on a single life or destiny. That is the pathos of our brief passages through the lives of others.

The other side of that blade, however, is profit—if not to them, then to us. They touched me. For the rest of my life, they are with me, in me, still teaching me. Their names—DeWayne, Jamal, Roman, Keeshawn—are still remembered by the coach whose name they have almost certainly forgotten. What a sublime irony!

Just when I think I have put them away from me like old toys, they pop out again to remind me of some rich lesson to be applied with a freshness that makes those young boys, as they were then, real again.

One relentlessly hot afternoon as they sullenly laced, strapped and snapped themselves into their antique football gear, the locker room filled with the customary jibes and remarkably creative quips so ubiquitous among ghetto gladiators. Suddenly one exchange rose above the others. Marcus, the quarterback, and Romeo, a massive, daunting tackle, squared off in the center of the dingy room. Leaving the relative safety of my "office," I quickly made my way toward them, hoping to save my quarterback's life.

Marcus was talented, fast and certainly the brightest player on the team. He was also renowned as the funniest "trash talker" in the city. Words rained upon poor Romeo in an unanswered torrential confluence of clever humor, obscenity and sarcasm. Speechless, mute, even brutish, Romeo, like a rhino in jockey shorts, let the river of Marcus's witticisms flow around him until at last he offered a response, memorable to me even now for its economy as well as its effect.

Seizing his massive purple helmet by its plastic face protector, he swung the lethal satellite without warning in an orbit defined by his fully extended trunklike arm and landed it with an odd thwack on Marcus's temple. The quarterback crumpled like an origami swan in the fist of a giant.

Staring down at the inert body of the quarterback at his feet, Romeo said, "Oh, yeah?"

For a man with dubious intellectual capacity and a limited vocabulary, Romeo held up his end of the argument well. Practice that day was a bit subdued. Marcus snoozed in the locker room, and no one, including the coach, felt inclined to explain to Romeo that "sticks and stones may break my bones, but words will never hurt me."

Since that day, however, I have longed for a biblical version of "Oh, yeah?" Satan and his minions, both flesh and spirit, are often cleverer, wittier and faster than I. In the face of demonic assault, accusation and a deluge of unanswerables from those men and demons who leave me argument-less and stupefied, I have longed for a word, some final, unstoppable "Oh, yeah?" to silence hell.

That word, that one great word is *nevertheless*.

There are times when this single word, *nevertheless*, is the full, perfect and sufficient answer. It can pull down vain philosophies, defeat devils and comfort the downtrodden. Altogether too often we squander time, energy and emotions trying to marshal intellectual explanations, when all we really need is one great word. At other times we wallow in guilt, labor under condemnation and stagger hopelessly on in the swamp of despair, when one word, the right word, rightly owned and rightly used, could lead us further in and higher up.

That word is *nevertheless.*

An unassuming word, easily dismissed as superfluous, it actually lends meaning to those sentences in which it resides and grace to the lips that learn it. *Nevertheless* is a word bridge connecting two ideas, the first of which has no power, even if it is factual, to lessen that greater truth of the second.

"Yesterday in class," a third-grader whined to his teacher, "you said that Tallahassee is the capital of Florida, but my father says it is Jacksonville."

"I'm sure he did," the weary teacher responds. "I have met your father, and nothing about that encounter encourages me to doubt you. I believe he said it—nevertheless, Tallahassee remains Florida's capital."

By mastering the strategic use of this powerful word we can build a firewall between truth and mere fact as well as opinion and error. *Nevertheless* says, "OK, that may be so, may be exactly as you have stated it, but it utterly lacks the strength to erode the unassailable truth it hopes to diminish."

"I own a chalet in Switzerland," boasts one business executive to another.

"I believe you are lying," his friend retorts.

"Nevertheless, I am not. The chalet is there, and I own it."

Nevertheless, that most economical and efficient of rebuttals, is the tool only of the utterly confident, the possessors of truths that could never, ever be lessened by anyone's opinions, objectives, philosophies or countering facts.

The strategic employment of *nevertheless* as it is modeled in Scripture, studied and mastered by believers, can usher in a joyful resurgence of faith and confident, victorious living. Learn where, when and how to use this one great word biblically, and in the face of life's most baffling circumstances you will never be defenseless.

One man told me he had learned how to always have the last word with his wife. No matter what she says, he answers, "Yes, dear."

Hmm. I'm not so sure that will work with every wife.

I am convinced, however, that there is a way for us to always have the last word with life and the devil. We can stand over Satan like Romeo above his locker-room tormentor and, in triumphant faith, say the word. Simply say the word—

NEVERTHELESS

1

THE NEVERTHELESS OF CHRIST
Luke 22:39–45

Howling demons dance around Him in His agony. Mind-torturing mental images rip at the edges of His soul. The knowledge of all that lies ahead rakes its steel claws across His naked nerves. Peace is shredded by the fast-approaching nightmare that lurks just ahead in the lonely darkness, not in some distant future, but at the very threshold of the moment.

The next few hours, horrific beyond imagining, lie unavoidably in His path. Sweeping Him toward a boiling cascade that will plunge Him into a demonic abyss, time, like a torrent, rages ahead. Minutes, just minutes. Seconds. Tick, tick, tick. Soon will come the hammer blows that will smash away the last of His self-possessed history and surrender Him to hell at the hands of others.

He prays, "O God, must I do this? Must I drain this evil cup? Take it away. Please, don't make Me drink this."

He looks between His own hands where they claw at the massive rock where He prays. Is it raining? No, it's blood, red and viscous on the boulder's unfeeling back. Blood? Is it raining blood? At His impending execution are sympathetic stars bleeding down upon the wretched stone?

At last He realizes the blood is His own, an emotion-hemorrhaged prefigurement of His impending death. The sweat-thickened blood exuding from His very pores marks the passing time. Tick, tick, drip, drip, drip.

The terrible moment approaches—climbing up from Kidron with torches visible above. They who would send Him down to Sheol come guided there by a friend. *Friend?* Where is one? All His friends lie sleeping behind Him, save the one who comes hither with murder in tow. Judas alone is awake and diligent. Judas was always the most diligent of them all.

He prays again. The same prayer: "Let this cup pass from my lips."

Then the demons do their worst. Having shown Him all the pain that awaits Him, having gleefully displayed for His fertile mind the humiliating picture of His own broken, naked form suspended cruelly for all to see, having done all to torture his imagination, they show Him the most horrible thing of all. My sins.

"Would You," the screaming devils demand of His poor wretched soul, "would You die for him?" My most depraved indifference, my blackest deeds, my lying tongue and arrogant, unbelieving self-worship paraded before His pleading soul must surely have been the worst torture of all.

To die, to sacrifice, to lay down one's life for the great or the good is one thing. To fling one's life into the sewer for perverted, twisted flesh so monstrously capacious for sin as to boggle heaven's mind, to die in horror's arms for a degenerate, hell-bent wretch is a reckless waste indeed.

He prays, "Let this cup pass from My lips."

Humanity's corporate whimper from beyond the veil of space and time is hardly audible there in Gethsemane's den of silence, and my own pathetic plea is surely lost. "Please, please, God, do not listen to Him. Please, Jesus, do not even ask to be excused from this Your dreadful destiny. If this cup passes from Your lips, it passes to ours where it belongs. We, I in particular, must drain its dregs eternally.

"You have seen the cross and Yourself nailed from that merciless frame, Lord Jesus. You have seen the sinful race for which You'll die, and looked full well upon this unworthy soul of mine. You have cried out to God for this cup to pass. Do You have anything else to say? 'Let this cup pass from my lips'? Is that Your last word?"

Satan shrieks, his laughter a scream from hell, but his question is the same as mine. "Will You toss away Your life for garbage such as this? You've asked that the cup pass from Your lips," Satan whispers in the Savior's ear. "Is that Your last word? Why squander all You are for such as him? Are You so great a fool? Look at him," Satan jeers at my depravity. "Look at them all. Do You expect them to repent, believe and obey? Most of them never will."

For once, Satan has told the truth. Most of them, us, will never, ever be anything but what we are, and we won't believe anything but our own self-deceptions.

The physical pain awaiting Him on the cross may well have been the least of it. He has known no sin. Never, not even for a second, has it separated Him from God. In perfect, submitted oneness with the Father, He has walked in sinless union, unbroken by the least offense.

But now, He knows that on the cross He must become all the sin that my race and I have done. Not merely bear the sin. *Become* the sin! What can that even mean?

He kneels, He prays and His fingers claw the stone while in His inner ears His own voice screams: "*Eli, Eli, lama sabachthani*…My God, my God, why hast thou forsaken me?" (Matt. 27:46).

To know and understand that He was to become my sin and receive in Himself the God-forsaken horror that was mine—that must have been the very worst of all.

At last, seeing all this and knowing what lies ahead of Him, Jesus lifts His eyes, lifts them above the filth of earth, above the blood-spattered rock on which He prays, and says the one word that will save a race that deserves no saving:

NEVERTHELESS

Jesus prays, and heaven and earth rejoice.

"Nevertheless…"—and hell's arguments are brought to nothing.

"Nevertheless…"—and the gap between the truth about God's redemptive love and me is eternally bridged.

In that one word, Jesus said so very much about His love and my sin. You see, He does not deny that I have sinned, that I am a sinner. He does not just paint over the reality of my unconscionable wickedness. He sees it, sees it all, for the unpardonable rebellion that it is. But, He says, as powerful as the stench of that sin is, it could never make God's will any less. Never, ever, ever the less.

With all the apparent weight on one side, the scales seem ready to tip in favor of Jesus' rejecting the cross. The preponderance of negatives includes the horror of the cross, the gall of dying for the unworthy, unbelieving and uncaring, all overlaying Jesus' very human instinct for self-preservation.

Then He says the one great word, the verbal fulcrum that renders most all argument to the contrary.

NEVERTHELESS

Despite all the rational arguments for life, Jesus chooses the cross. Knowing everything, all that lies ahead, all my sin, all of humanity's depravity, knowing that His own friends would deny and desert Him, Jesus chooses the cross with the one great word.

Remember the definition? *Nevertheless* is a bridge between two opposing ideas or sets of facts, the first of which cannot invalidate or even dilute the latter, cannot ever make it less true.

Jesus said, "I see all the agony of the cross and the grave, and my impulse is to avoid it. Nevertheless…"

Why? What came after that great word? What truth so transcends all the weight before it as to mute its strident tones with just one word?

"…*Thy will be done.*"

On the one side, an ineluctable mass of reason denounces the cross as insanity. Yet on the other, one truth alone outweighs all human arguments, vanity and despair—the loving will of God the Father Almighty. Jesus stands astride that cosmic rift, the accumulated arguments of the world, the devil and His own flesh on one side, and nothing but His Father's will on the other. Sinful, doomed humanity hangs in the balance.

NEVERTHELESS

With that one word, Jesus freed us from damnation and revealed the love of God. Jesus was not, as some would seem to imply, saving us *from God*. God was in Christ, saving us *from us*. It is in response to the reconciling love of God the Father that Jesus says, "Nevertheless."

The cross is at the very heart of the Father. That is why Jesus is called "the Lamb slain from the foundation" (Rev. 13:8). All my insecurities are swallowed up in the knowledge of so great a Father's love. I do not have to discern God's will for my eternal disposition. Jesus saw it, yielded to it, surrendered to it and embraced the cross that I might go free. I do not have to wonder if God loves me. It was God's love for me that outweighed a battalion of shrieking demons and all my sinful self.

It was for me that God sent His Son. "I know what he is and what he has done," the Father told the Word, "but he's My child, and I want him here with Me. Take up that for which You were born—that cross, that nightmare of the soul that should by all justice be his—and let him come to Me."

"By Your will and preordained mysterious purpose, I am flesh, and that flesh cries out to be excused," Christ answered in Gethsemane.

Please, Lord, oh, please look beyond my fault and see the Father's will.

I do.

Please, do not pray for the cup to pass from You.

I do not want to drink.

Don't You have anything else to say?

Yes, I do.

Say it, Lord. Just one great word and I shall live.

NEVERTHELESS

Nevertheless. Word of words. Free at last. With that one word, the Son has set us free.

2

THE NEVERTHELESS OF THE UNSHAKABLE FOUNDATION

2 Timothy 2:19

Armed with education, intellect and ravenous appetites to overthrow and devour the faith of defenseless lambs, the wolves of humanism run in packs.

Cowardly for the most part, they position themselves on liberal university campuses and in creative communities where pluralism is sacrosanct and tolerance a god. There they wait for the innocent and unprepared to wander away from their protective fold. They attack with philosophies like incisors and mockery for claws. Ferocious, relentless and remorseless, they camouflage their lupine anti-Christian ferocity behind an exterior of urbane sophistication, which is the very quintessence of the intolerant hypocrisy they love to blame on Christians and claim to despise.

Charm, wit and fashion—all of preeminent importance to them—become weapons in their hands. They use them to intimidate impressionable youth and smother creative expressions of faith. Evangelical iconoclasts are fair game, even as these so-called liberals mouth an unending mantra of inclusiveness and free thought.

Students, dinner guests and visiting authors who speak for amorality and sexual perversion are celebrated as alternative voices well worthy of the civil protection afforded by the free speech so valued in the west. But youthful Christians are lacerated without pity. Evidently liberalism's pluralistic elasticity only stretches to the left.

In such an antagonistic atmosphere, believers, particularly young believers, need an untrumpable ace. Where ontological arguments fail and apologetics prove effete, there must be some irrefutable, some unanswerable that dismisses adversaries and buttresses faith. That ultimate answer, which, by the way, infuriates unbelievers, is found in the clear, calm syllables of…

NEVERTHELESS

You may find yourself at the ragged end of your own intellect and bereft of defenses against those who have honed their arguments to a fine edge. Remember they are their father's children. From the Garden of Eden, he has been Apollyon, the Destroyer and the Confuser. Do not be overly discouraged that his children, the sons of darkness, are better at destruction than you seem to be at defense.

Also, do not feel the need to be smarter and better educated than humanists who have made intellect and education their god. This is not to grant permission to be ignorant and utterly without apologetics. It is simply to say that no matter how bright you are and regardless of how well prepared are your arguments, you may eventually come up against a brighter and better-prepared atheist. That is proof of absolutely nothing except the old Texas axiom: "There's never been a horse that couldn't be rode and never a cowboy that couldn't be throwed."

Anyway, if you will rest yourself in the ultimate answer that is yours and learn when and how to use it, you will never be defeated by vain philosophies.

Wait until they have spent all their energy, used up all their intellectual ammunition and stand, at last, triumphant over what they expect to be your whimpering, defeated form. Wait until they finish. "There," they will crow, "what do you have to say about that?"

"Just one word," you answer with no hint of shrill panic in your voice.

NEVERTHELESS

"What?" the question comes. "What did you say?" It is not an answer, but a question. The confuser is genuinely confused.

"I said, 'Nevertheless.'"

"Nevertheless?"

"Yes. After all your arguments. Despite your obvious

intellect, which is enviable. At the end of all that you or anyone can say, the foundation of the Lord standeth sure. You cannot change it, erode it or tear it down, nor need I defend it. Indeed, I am obviously not equipped to do so. Nevertheless, the foundation of the Lord standeth sure."

Lord, these people are smarter than I am.

Yes, but they are not smarter than I AM.

Yes, but they can't see You.

They will.

They don't believe in You.

They will.

Meanwhile, what do I say? I am out of arguments.

Good.

Now, what do I say?

Say what I say. Nevertheless.

Likewise, when events, terrible events threaten to overwhelm you and rip at the very foundation of your soul, remember that you still have an answer. "Nevertheless, the foundation of the Lord standeth sure."

You see, we want to believe that all the bad stuff happens to others, bad others mostly, but reality is quite different. In fact, the Bible nowhere promises us a pain-free life of pure blessing, or that the wicked alone will suffer. The rain falls on the just and the unjust.

What do we say then? How can we answer when Satan laughs and mocks in the waiting room of the intensive care unit? When he and his demons dance around us in our brokenhearted, benumbed grief and demand an answer? What answer is there when there is no answer?

"Nevertheless, the foundation of the Lord standeth sure."

No argument, no circumstance, no soul-torturing loss can change that. In defeat, in famine, in brokenness and in death, that one answer practiced over a lifetime and uttered at propitious moments is the victory.

When you stand by the bed of loved ones and watch in futility as they gasp for breath around the telltale rattle in their throat, death's mask already visible on their face, Satan will gladly stand on the other side of the bed. Oh, yes, he makes hospital calls. "Now," he will whisper, "now, what do you say? Now, what is your answer to this?"

Grip the altar with both hands, and to this as well, speak with a confidence, wounded but not undone:

NEVERTHELESS

In the verses that precede 2 Timothy 2:19, Paul memorializes the erroneous teachings of Hymeneus and Philetus, who apart from their blasphemy were utterly forgettable. In his customary subtlety, Paul denounces them as "gangrene" in the church and their doctrine as "profane and vain babblings."

Paul does not, however, lightly dismiss their error as being without consequences. Such vain babblings "overthrew the faith of some," and Paul, never one to mince words, lays the blame squarely at the door of Hymeneus and Philetus.

There will always be among us such gangrenous characters as Hymeneus and Philetus. Unfortunately, they will occasionally overthrow the faith of some. But neither the gangrene of their false doctrine nor the tragic loss of those thus overthrown changes anything eternal. Paul's answer to blasphemers was a broadside directly at Satan's waterline. His was a succinct, powerful and perfect answer.

To all the naysayers, to the clever atheists, to the eloquent and the damned, to your own despairing soul, to your aching heart, to all the crumpled hopes, shattered dreams and gut-wrenching disappointments, you still have all the answer you need.

Nevertheless the foundation of the Lord standeth sure.

—2 Timothy 2:19

3

THE NEVERTHELESS OF
A HARD THING

2 Kings 2:10

Gathering clouds. Portentous and dark. The rain is coming. They all made such judgments in the natural realm quite frequently. They knew how it felt, how the weather told about itself and informed the observant about the future.

How that happened in the spiritual dimension was a bit murkier. The gathering clouds were certainly there. Many, independently of each other, had been sensing them. Elisha saw the clouds first and most clearly. Saw is the wrong word. Sensed? That's not much better. Anyway, other prophets soon became aware of the spiritual climate gathering itself for some great movement. But what did it all mean?

Praying, waiting, listening in intense prophetic communities at Gilgal, Jericho and elsewhere, they strained their ears for the words upon the wind. Something was about to happen. They knew that—but what?

Elisha again heard it first. His master was going to God. Elisha knew it, smelled the coming rain, wet and cool upon the breeze. The great man himself, Elijah, had finished his work. God was going to...what? Take him? What did that mean? Elisha knew only that Elijah was soon to be with God. And if he knew it, soon the sons of the prophets across Israel would know it. Was his the only nose that could smell rain?

Elijah said nothing, the future seeming to hang between them in the air, more real than the present. Two prophets avoiding each other's eyes like guilty boys who, having eaten stolen melon, do not know how to talk about it.

"You stay here," Elijah said at last. "The Lord has called me to Bethel. Wait here. I will go there alone."

"As the Lord lives," Elisha said, "I will not stay here. I will not let you out of my sight."

Elijah soberly eyed his disciple but said nothing. A nod, a shrug, nothing more, and the elder prophet rose and turned his face toward Bethel. As they walked, not a word passed between them, but occasionally, more frequently with each mile, Elisha would turn his head just enough to see his master's craggy profile.

At Bethel a troubled knot of prophets gathered around Elisha and pulled him aside. Elijah still said nothing, but he stared at the sky as if...what? What?!

"Do you know..." the prophets clucked like old maids with a juicy tidbit of gossip to peck at. "The Lord will take away your covering today. Elijah will..."

"Shush," Elisha scolded them. "Hold your peace. Of course, I know. Is the God who speaks at Bethel silent at Gilgal?"

The problem with prophets in community, Elisha thought, *is that they degenerate into beehives of spiritual gossip, bustling with whisperings of "Have you heard?" and "Do you know?" Prophets in swarms quickly become widows and old maids,* he thought, *hangers-on at funerals and the last to leave the women's well.*

"Jericho," Elijah said when Elisha rejoined him, leaving the Bethel prophets to dither. "I must go down to Jericho, but you stay here. Chat with them. You must be weary of an old man's company."

"My answer has not changed," Elisha said firmly enough to get a raised eyebrow from his master. "As the Lord lives, I will not leave you."

At Jericho the prophets were already in a buzz. "Do you know…?" Did they think him deaf to the wind, to the Voice? "Today," one added. "Elijah will be taken today."

"Hold your peace," Elisha scolded them. They drew back, but gazed with sidelong glances and whispered among themselves.

"Tarry here," Elijah said. "I must go down to the Jordan. The Lord hath sent me to the river."

"I am staying with you. Do you understand? Nothing can distract me today."

"We shall see."

At the river Elijah used his cloak to slap at the water's surface almost casually, and it ruptured instantly like melon split by an axe. The hair at the back of Elisha's neck prickled, and his skin tingled. Soon. Very soon. Rain on the breeze. The Voice grew louder.

"Ask what you will," Elijah said. "We both know what is about to happen. What shall I do for you before I am taken away?"

"Let a double portion of thy spirit be upon me."

"Thou hast asked a hard thing."

Elisha was shocked. Never, not once in all their journeys had he ever heard Elijah speak of a "hard thing." Blinding an army, praying down fire, sealing up heaven—none of these had been "hard things." Not even toppling the house of Ahab had been a "hard thing." But a double portion was a "hard thing."

"Nevertheless," Elijah said, "if you see me when I am taken up, you shall have it. Look away, and you shall not. Let us walk a bit further on. Talk with me one last time."

Suddenly, straight at them, terrifying and irresistible, galloped a chariot and four horses, all ablaze. They were not of natural substance on fire. They *were* fire. The rig drove between the two men like a lightning bolt, but Elisha's eyes were riveted on Elijah. Don't look away! Don't look away! Forget the chariot. Watch the master.

The breeze became a Wind and the Voice a roar. A cyclone of whirling power engulfed Elijah, and he rose, higher, higher, fading, hidden by the tornado's fury.

"Elijah!" he wailed. "My father!"

No wind and no voice comforted Elisha. Silence. Deafening silence. Then he saw it. A puddle of plain cloth. The spore of prophetic greatness. A soft, fabric fossil of the rugged giant gone up in a whirlwind. The mantle of Elijah. Dare he? He had asked a hard thing. What was it Elijah had said?

NEVERTHELESS

Retrieving the cloak, Elisha turned to face the Jordan and the knot of prophets peering at him across the stream. This was it. Hard prayer or not, he must know. From deep within himself, from some passion point of furious faith, a cry hurled itself up from Elisha's soul toward heaven.

"Where is the God of Elijah?"

Spontaneously, in a prophet's instinct, he lashed the waiting waters with Elijah's mantle. In that motion the mantle became his, for the river burst apart. Elisha walked back to Jericho's waiting prophets, returning exactly as he and Elijah had left.

"The spirit of Elijah! The spirit of Elijah rests on Elisha," cried the prophets.

Elisha had indeed asked a hard thing. A double portion of Elijah's spirit? A very hard thing…

NEVERTHELESS

"Don't you think that's asking a bit much?" How many times I've heard that! Yet a fear of asking too much causes many believers to ask too little. The scriptural evidence indicates that God is more impatient with the timid than with the aggressive.

> Let us therefore come boldly unto the throne of grace…
>
> —HEBREWS 4:16

Not here alone in the story of his mantling, but throughout his ministry, Elisha understood the value of asking "hard things." Even as he lay dying, Elisha was visited by a weeping King Joash (2 Kings 13:14–21). Discerning that the king's tears were in part grief and in part fear of the Syrians without Elisha's prophetic presence, the man of God told the king to shoot an arrow out the window.

That, Elisha explained after the king obeyed, was the arrow of the Lord's deliverance from Syria. Elisha assumed that Joash would realize this was a prophetic moment, a supernatural combination of word, act and faith.

"Now," Elisha said, "take the other arrows and strike the ground." Joash did, three times, and Elisha was angry and horrified.

"You should have hit more times. Why stop at three? Why not five? Why not six? Now," Elisha explained, "you will only defeat the Syrians three times. You should have kept on hitting until you received all the victory you wanted."

Most do not strike enough, do not seek, cry out, pray or ask big enough. Elisha obviously felt that his prophetic statement, "This is the arrow of the Lord's deliverance from Syria," should have made it clear to Joash that God was up to something.

Many times believers miss the prophetic moment because of insensitivity, dullness or distraction and ask too little. When God says hit—HIT—and keep on hitting. Does that deep prayer of your heart seem massively unanswerable? So was a double portion of the anointing of the greatest prophet of his day.

NEVERTHELESS

Here are some key insights about asking hard things:

1. Be sensitive to the right "hard thing." Solomon asked for wisdom, Jabez for blessing, Caleb for an entire mountain and Elisha for anointing. Let God birth "hard things" in your spirit and get ready to ask. (See 1 Kings 3; 1 Chronicles 4:10; Joshua 14; 2 Kings 2.)

2. Be sensitive to the right moment of God. A divine door to the inner throne room will spring open, and you will sense this is the

moment to ask that "hard thing." Elijah asked, "What shall I do for thee?" Ask! Without hesitation, seize the moment in faith.

3. Do not be distracted. Ask most Bible readers, and they will tell you Elijah went up to heaven in a chariot of fire. Not so. The chariot was to separate the men and test Elisha's concentration. If Elisha's eyes had followed the flamboyant vision of the fiery chariot and its flaming steeds, he would have missed Elijah going up in a whirlwind. Remember, as exciting as is the chariot of fire, if you let your eyes, mind and faith wander from the focus of your prayer, you may well miss the whirlwind to follow. The desire of Elisha's hard prayer concerned Elijah's anointing. The chariot of fire did not relate. Elijah was the focus. "If thou see me when I am taken…" Elijah said. That "if" in a "hard thing" is huge. Stay focused.

4. Remember that the very term *hard thing* is human. What could be "harder" or "easier" to God? Was it "harder" for God to make an elephant than a mouse? Is one disease "harder" for God to heal than another?

Ask "hard things" remembering that God is pleased with faith, not intimidated by big prayers. "Thou hast asked a hard thing…" was Elijah's view. "Thou hast asked a hard thing…" may well have been a compliment to Elisha's faith rather than a complaint about his prayer.

Regardless, the word of God through Elijah was certainly clear.

NEVERTHELESS

Ask Me.

Lord, You mean ask, and apologize for asking.

Just ask.

Lord, we never want to be too bold.

Be bold. Please, won't someone be bold?

We don't want to strain You.

What?

Sorry. *Impossible* looks like a big word to us.

It is a big word. But there is a bigger one.

What, Lord?

NEVERTHELESS

4

THE NEVERTHELESS OF VICTORY

2 Samuel 5:1–7; 1 Chronicles 11:4–9

David. A complicated, multiple-warhead genius who can excel—not just get by—but really blow the competition away in a variety of disparate disciplines comes maybe once in a generation. Such was King David. He was a poet to rival Shakespeare, a military genius at the level of Patton, musician, composer, mystic and, not least of all, consummate politician.

When at the end of a long and bloody civil war, he was, at last, anointed king over a united nation, David knew that Hebron must be left behind for Judah, his kinsmen. Through the long internecine bloodbath, Hebron had been perfect as a capital. But not for a new nation, not for a united Israel. A tribal capital is just that. David knew if he stayed at Hebron, all the other tribes would never grasp his vision of a renewed, united Jewish state.

Yet, which of the other tribal centers would work any better? The politician in David knew that a new nation needed a new capital. Tribal Hebrews must learn to think of themselves as national Israelis. Saul, the first king, had ruled from Gibeah of Benjamin because he was of the tribe of Benjamin. Everyone expected David to set up court in Hebron of Judah.

Such a grand gesture as a new and neutral capital would make the needed political statement in no uncertain terms. David would be seen as the king of all the people. Not twelve capitals for twelve tribes, but a national capital for a unified nation. Such a city would be the national center for Hebrew religion and government. But where? David accepted the oil of anointing, set up "temporary" government in Hebron and started the hard, bloody work of driving the Jebusites, Philistines and others from his burgeoning nation as he waited for God's answer. Not just any city would do. A king of God's own choosing must reign from the city of God's own choosing.

Seven years later, only the impregnable Jebusite fortress at Jebus had eluded the edge of David's sword. This stronghold had resisted every attack with notable ease. Massive, unapproachable and easily defended, Jebus alone, of all the Jebusite cities, defied David.

"Our city is so strong," the Jebusites boasted, "that even the weakest among us can defend it."

When David's emissaries called on the main Jebusite army at Jebus to surrender, their answer was galling.

"You are surrounded," David's spokesman called up to the city wall. "Why go through a siege and lose anyway? David will enter the city sooner or later. Surrender and live."

"Our blind and lame can defend this city," the Jebusites

laughed. "Until he takes away the blind and the lame, David cannot come in here."

"I fear they are right, Your Majesty," an officer whispered discreetly to King David.

"Perhaps," David mused. "Perhaps."

"It would take a miracle to conquer Jebus," another officer muttered darkly.

At this David seemed to brighten considerably. "Truly? Then this may be the place."

"What place?"

"The city I've been looking for, for seven years."

"Look at those walls, Sire," wailed a young captain. "This city will not fall. It simply will not fall."

"I heard a word from the Lord," David whispered.

They all leaned close. "What word, Your Majesty?"

NEVERTHELESS

Jebus was an impregnable fortress city, the fortified garrison capital of a warrior nation. The soldiers within its walls were not blind and lame, but even if they had been, they could have kept David out. They had a water supply, the high ground, fortifications; time was on their side, not favoring the Israelis living outside in tents.

It is notable that in both the Chronicles version of the fall of Jebus and in Samuel's account, the significant word is *nevertheless* (2 Sam. 5:7; 1 Chron. 11:5).

There are some wonderful lessons for life and leadership in David's conquest of Jebus. The first is a word to every believer. With every new opportunity will come both change and challenge. David knew it. Hebron was acceptable for awhile, but he foresaw the day when change would come. David waited on the divine moment and welcomed the change. He neither hurried nor hated it.

Remember, you may be able to be a king or stay at Hebron, but you may not be able to do both for very long. Accept and embrace the inevitability of change as a necessary implication of advancement, but wait on God's guidance. Rushing or reluctance may cost you equally.

Second, notice that the new "opportunity" may be fraught with daunting challenges. When you are not the king, the Jebusites are someone else's problem. Put on the crown, and your heavy head must find the solution. At Hebron there is no unconquerable opposition. March on Jebus, and the battle is on. You can have security at Hebron with little chance of a glorious victory. You can win a great victory at Jebus, but not while you sit warm and cozy at Hebron.

Third, and greatest of all, there is no chance for a miracle until one is needed. There is no hope for a magnificent victory until there are unbeatable odds. The weak and fearful look up at the looming walls of Jebus and see certain defeat. The faith-filled see the moment of God. Cowards mutter words of doubt and despair.

Conquerors say, "Nevertheless."

David was not mindless of the reality before him. Jebus was there, was obviously unbeatable, easily defended even by the blind and lame. Denial is not, as some have thought, the same as faith. Catalog the strengths of Jebus. List the reasons that it cannot fall. Go on; be real. Then having done so, say the word that conquers the unconquerable.

"Nevertheless...as Jebus fell, so shall this that stands before me."

Satan wants to convince you of the utter futility of your faith as well as your plan. He will gladly point out any of the strengths of Jebus that you have not already noticed—the height of the walls, the strength of the gates and the power of the opposing army.

Satan is eager to explain the hopelessness of your situation: That addiction can never be overcome. No church has ever grown in this town. The gang violence in this neighborhood is unstoppable. The financial situation is irreversible. All these are but variations on "the blind and the lame could defend Jebus. David will not come in."

In the face of insurmountable odds, superior strength and supernatural opposition, use the word of David. After all that Satan can do and say to convince you of your own defeat, remind him of his at Jebus.

Finally, remember that the secret of the fall of Jebus may well be a creative approach visible only to the eyes of faith. Fear blinds many to answers, but when faced with a challenge from which reason recoils, there is, just behind *nevertheless*, an answer. Hidden in one of Jebus's strengths was the answer to David's victory, and David saw it.

Jebus's citizens felt secure in an extended siege because of their water source. From Mt. Zion, where the fortress stood, down to the spring at Gihon was a hidden water shaft. No matter how long the siege lasted, Jebus would have water. But where others saw this as Jebus's strength, David saw it as all the vulnerability he needed.

> Whosoever getteth up to the gutter, and smiteth
> the Jebusites, and the lame and the blind...he shall
> be chief and captain.
>
> —2 SAMUEL 5:8

In any great undertaking there will always be Job's friends to tell you what is impossible, impractical and that this, whatever it is, will be the death of you. It may or may not even be genuine concern for your well-being. Jealousy, envy and hidden agendas can turn concerned associates into angry obstructionists.

When Nehemiah returned to Jerusalem and announced his God-inspired intention to rebuild Jerusalem's walls, Sanballet and Tobiah mocked him bitterly (Neh. 4:2). They verbally abused Nehemiah's great dream in four ways:

1. The Jews were too feeble for the work.

2. They could not even fortify themselves, let alone the city walls.

3. There were no resources. The material from previous walls had been burned beyond usefulness.

4. It was futile to try. "Even if you succeed a little at first," they said, "it will come to nothing."

There will always be someone at your elbow to tell you how unachievable your dream is. Such voices of discouragement are a dime a dozen. Why give them any credibility? Wise counsel that helps you analyze costs, risks and potential return is valuable, but weak and jealous little people whose own dreams have died want nothing more than to kill yours.

Nehemiah, like David, saw what they could not. They saw burned stones and heaps of useless rubbish. Nehemiah saw mighty walls. His detractors saw a weak and conquered people. Nehemiah saw a worthy work of restoration and renewal.

Nehemiah, like David, knew just the word for such an impossible task and an army of opposition.

"Nevertheless," he wrote, "we made our prayer unto our God, and set a watch against them day and night, because of them" (Neh. 4:9).

Besieged by angry critics who, having seen their own dreams die, despise yours? Your one-word way to victory is a path of faith and due diligence. Make your prayer to your God, and then keep Tobiah and Sanballet away.

There is a small church in a metal building perched rather precariously on the shoulder of a winding mountain road in the south. It is not even in the city limits of the nearest town, if you dare call the cluster of crude houses, rustic grocery and antique post office a town. Yet the sign out front reads, "World Outreach Center."

At first I chuckled smugly at the brazenness of such a name. What ostentation! What idiotic presumption. World Outreach Center, indeed. Then it dawned on me. Someone in there is seeing what I cannot, dreaming beyond the obvious and refusing to be discouraged by the likes of me.

What a name.

I kind of like it.

You do? Really?

Really. It sort of reminds me of what I said My people should be doing.

Lord, is that You?

I alone give dreams. Satan has no dreams and cannot birth them. Do you not see a dream in the name on that sign?

You have to admit, it is a bit grandiose.

Nevertheless.

Yes, Lord. I bless them and their dream in Your name.

That's more like it.

When the battle for Jebus was over and David stood victorious on Mt. Zion, he made the stunning announcement that Jebus was to be renamed Jerusalem and become the new capital city.

What had been an unconquerable Jebusite stronghold became the Holy City named in prayer, memorialized in song, longed for in the Diaspora and rebuilt over and over again by the people of God.

The men and officers of David's army had seen the conquest of Jebus as impossible, while David was already seeing a new city for a new nation. They beheld Jebus's unassailable fortifications and saw certain defeat. David looked at a water shaft and saw certain victory.

Jebus was unbeatable.

NEVERTHELESS

Jerusalem is and Jebus is no more.

5

The Nevertheless of Obedience

Luke 5:5

Jesus' command seemed like mockery to the sweating, exhausted fisherman. It was broad daylight. Even this carpenter should know you cannot catch fish on the Lake of Tiberius in broad daylight. Peter had labored all night—when fish are to be caught—hauling the heavy wet nets until his back muscles screamed. He had often noticed that empty nets are heavier than full ones. Having fished when it was possible to catch fish, now, in the daylight, should he work when it was patently impossible?

Then there were the people on the shoreline. The lake was not so broad that they could not easily see the boat and the fisherman and the mysterious passenger. Peter knew that he would look foolish if he cast the nets out upon the sunlit waters. He could just hear them laughing, calling out their taunts to him across the sun-splashed waves and fishes. Peter hated being laughed at.

Anyway, he was tired, very tired and discouraged, and not at all inclined to indulge the nonsensical whims of itinerate rabbis. Was it not *his* boat, his back and his time?

Was this disquieting Nazarene going to help? Peter thought not. The visitor so casually tossing off directions, as if He knew anything about fishing, seemed to care nothing for Peter's aching muscles. And what about that? Did Peter not have the right to be fatigued, fatigued beyond expression, and hungry to boot? Could not a weary fisherman just go home and eat and sleep away the fruitless night without being told how to fish by would-be prophets from landlocked villages?

All right. All right! He would do it. But not without pointing out the idiocy of it loudly enough so that everyone on the bank would know this was not his idea. All right. This carpenter wants nets—He'll get nets, wet, heavy, empty nets in broad daylight. If that's what He wants, that's what He will get.

"We have fished all night, Lord, and taken nothing," Peter explained, barely managing to keep the rebellion in his heart from ringing in his tone. How should he acquiesce? He needed a word to get him over the hump of his unspoken resistance and on into obedience. *Nevertheless…* Did he let condescension creep in? He hoped not. Mournful, exhausted, reluctant doubt? Well, maybe a little. Whatever lurked in the recesses of his heart, the word still came out. "Nevertheless, at thy word, I will let down the nets."

There, it was said. Now, let it be done. Hurling the cast net out to spread and splash weblike and unpromising on the lake's sparkling azure surface, Peter smiled patiently at the rabbi whose troubling eyes remained fixed on Peter's broad, weathered face. Neither said anything as the net sank down, leaving diamonds of light dancing on the surface. Fishing in the day! That shows what carpenters and rabbis know about it.

Peter gathered the draw cord to pull the net closed and began to haul it in, not easily as he expected but with backbreaking effort. It couldn't be. As the net surfaced, the sun played on the boiling fish like laughter, dancing with delight upon the little bodies madly trying to flip free of each other and the net. He was stunned. Never, not on his greatest night of fishing, had Peter ever made a haul like this. This was not natural; this was…

He glanced over his shoulder at the rabbi. Was He smiling? Was that a glint in His eyes or just the sun? Bounty is bounty, Peter decided. He had seen no sense in this daylight fishing. Nevertheless, this was a week's work done in one haul. Yes, that's it exactly.

NEVERTHELESS

We often labor under the burdensome illusion that all obedience must be joyful. "Be crucified upside down? Oh, thank You, Lord. Gladly, Lord. Ha, ha, what could be better?" Don't be absurd. There are places to which He leads or calls us, burdens He may ask us to heft and obligations so strenuous that they make no more sense to us than fishing in the daylight did to Peter.

It is, despite what they say, permissible to explain things to God. He will not be angry. Apparently Jesus did not understand the situation, and Peter took pains to clarify it for Him. You can, too. God will let you talk. He is sovereign, not rude.

"Lord, this church is not the right one for me. I need a growing congregation in an upscale neighborhood." "Lord, I know You said to invite my neighbor to church, but he is an atheist, a very dislikable and grumpy jerk of an atheist." "Lord, I know You said to forgive my mother-in-law, but You have not met my mother-in-law." "Stand up and walk? Can't You see, Lord, that my legs are twisted and useless?"

God is big. He is neither destroyed nor dissuaded by our objections, complaints and explanations. Tell Him all about it. Surely the subtle nuances of the problem are wasted on Him. From His profoundly limited vantage point, God certainly cannot see the ramifications so obvious to you. Let Him hear it all. I'm sure He will appreciate the help.

When you are completely finished, however, and He just sits there in the other end of the boat staring at you, a decision must be made. God will listen, but He will never argue. He just sits there trailing His finger in the water while He studies your face. He has told you what to do. You have told Him why it makes no sense. Now, what do you say?

NEVERTHELESS

The *nevertheless* of naked obedience unlocks more miracles than we can imagine. The bridge between our discouragement and God's will is *nevertheless,* and on the other side are the bulging nets of His bounty.

C. T. Studd was in his fifties, sickly and burdened with an invalid wife. No missions board in England would even entertain the idea of his going into the most dangerous part of Africa. Studd and his wife, Priscilla, had labored in India, and by all logic deserved a rest in England. But Studd heard God calling him to Central Africa.

Unmapped, largely unsettled, violent and rife with tropical diseases, Central Africa in the nineteenth century was considered a "missionary's graveyard." Even if God were to call someone there, it would surely not be an aging, infirm Englishman without the support of a missions board. God would certainly never call him to leave his bedridden wife in England to pray and write letters and raise financial support.

Studd's response? *Nevertheless.* Studd did go, and God did supply, and revival did come to the African interior. He did not see his wife for twelve years. He was frequently criticized, highly controversial and mightily used of God.

There is another reality that lies wonderfully waiting just behind this nevertheless of obedience. We must not make it the central issue, but it is part of the whole matter. Blessings. Miraculous, supernatural, abundant blessings await the nets of the bone-weary who will, despite all, throw one more cast precisely as told.

When Peter pulled up the nets, they were miraculously filled. Peter immediately recognized it as a miraculous draught and was more open than ever before to hear a word of destiny. This is not to say that we should try to hold God to a bargain. "All right, I'll obey, but these nets better be full!"

Nonsense! He speaks; we obey—period. Having said that, however, it must be added that obedience unlocks miracles. The walls of Jericho did not fall by the faith in Joshua's heart alone, but also by the faith in his feet and in the feet of an army. Frequently, the more unlikely the command, the greater the miracle.

Do not look at the sun on the lake or at the improbability of the catch. Look beneath the surface. See with the eyes of faith, and throw out the net. First comes *nevertheless*. Then comes the miracle.

There will come a point, sometimes an excruciating painful point, where we, in one end of the boat, will stare into the steady eyes of Christ as He sits calmly in the other end and summons us to acts of obedience, ministry or sacrifices that fly in the face of all natural reason. These will never be the mad impulses of the emotionally unbalanced. Some lamebrain with a religious spirit will occasionally wade out to his death and leave a note on the shore claiming God told him to walk on water. That's not the nevertheless of faith, but of presumption.

When, like C. T. Studd, mature, seasoned saints have wrestled through and gotten a word from God, when they have said it all, argued with God, offered up all their objections and God is still steadfast, then only one word will serve to move from reluctance to action. Remember, you do not have to understand it or relish it, or even like it. You just have to cast the net anyway.

Been hearing from God for a tough and seemingly unrealistic task? Be of good comfort. You are in good company. Moses was a speech-impaired octogenarian when God called him back to Egypt where there was a price on his head. Abraham was a married man with obligations when God called him to leave it all without even knowing the destination. David Wilkerson was the pastor of a rural church with no inner-city experience when God called him to work with gangs in New York City. Father Damien was a healthy young priest under no church obligation when God told him to live among lepers where he contracted the disease and died. And no one, not even a nun named Theresa, wanted to care for the filthy, terminally ill wretches of India. Why would God waste her energies on the dying when the living are so needy?

Lord, Peter was different from us.

No, he wasn't.

He wasn't? What about Joshua? He was different, right?

Wrong.
Paul?
Nope.
Elijah?
Just like you.
Well, why did they get all these miracles?
Because when I commanded, they answered.
What did they say, Lord?

NEVERTHELESS

When you are too tired, too old, too young, impoverished or bound up by obligations to obey a calling of God, let Him hear all about it. Tell Him about your long, dark night of fruitless fishing. Tell Him that your back hurts and your arms are sore, and that, anyway, fish don't bite in the daytime on your particular lake and that you are surprised He doesn't know that. Tell Him all that.

Then look into His wonderful, calm, unruffled eyes and say:

"Nevertheless, at Thy word..."

6

THE NEVERTHELESS OF MINISTRY

2 Timothy 1:12

Blind and frail, her wiry, white hair stirred ever so slightly by a faint, hot breeze, the old German missionary came slowly toward me. She could not have possibly known I was there with two Africans watching her tap her way slowly across the baked, grassless "lawn" of the guesthouse.

"Who is she?" I asked.

"Bible translator. Now she has river blindness."

"She will die?"

"Yes. She will die. She is going back to Germany. She will die there."

"What did she do here?" I asked.

"She put the Bible into two languages."

"All by herself?"

"All by herself."

"Now she goes home to die in Germany."

"All by herself."

The unfairness, the lonely, blind, painful unfairness of it swamped me. I stood there slowly sinking into a bottomless marsh of injustice. She should have been on a dais at a head table, receiving honors and applause and the undying gratitude of thousands. A sightless Lufthansa flight and a few months unvisited in a ward where impoverished old ladies die seemed the wrong ending for a holy life full of great kingdom accomplishments.

Then, as though I could hear her thoughts—or were they God's?—I seemed to find relief, even joy, in that one great word…

NEVERTHELESS

"For the which cause I have suffered these things: *nevertheless* I am not ashamed: for I know whom I have believed, and am persuaded that he is able to keep that which I have committed unto him against that day."

The Bible nowhere promises Christ's ambassadors some rose-petaled aisleway of safety through suffering. Indeed, scriptures such as Psalm 34:19 say the exact opposite: "Many are the afflictions of the righteous…" We will, even the most righteous among us, "suffer these things," as Paul says.

However we try to impose upon God our limited human fairness doctrines, He will not submit. The mother of three must have three identical candy bars or none at all. If she has only one, it must be divided equally, with a ruler, while all three *kibitz*. We cannot imagine that mother standing her youngest before the other two and, without apparent merit, awarding him alone candy.

"Watch," she admonishes the two candy-bar-less siblings. "Look how your brother relishes that gooey chocolate. See the obvious delight in his eyes, the salacious way he licks his lips. Rejoice with him and be glad."

Yet that is precisely what God does. He lifts one to prominence and public blessing, plants his feet in a broad place and anoints his ministry before the eyes of the world. Another pours out his life in the jungle, and the Peruvian Air Force shoots down his plane, killing his wife and child. Ministry, hardship, suffering, blessing, miracles, signs, wonders and unspeakable agony seem all jumbled in the fruit basket of life, which defies our cozy explanations and tidy little formulas of faith.

Only one word will make sense of it all, bring a victorious joyful meaning to it, for that word scatters the midnight of temporal confusion with the dawn of eternal significance.

NEVERTHELESS

Satan has practiced his arguments, learned his lines well, and never misses an opportunity to plunge the dagger deep into the soft, defenseless tissue of our pain.

"You see," he says, "there is your God for you. You see how He is. He lets you work like a slave, pour out your heart, preach till you drop, pray without ceasing, and He rewards you with a church split, angry elders and rabid sheep tearing your flesh to shreds. Do you deny these facts?"

"No."

"Are you or are you not suffering?" Satan asks.

"I am."

"Well, what do you have to say to this fine mess?" he mocks.

NEVERTHELESS

If our wounded confusion is on one side of this grand word, what is on the other? We stand unmoved on *nevertheless*. The weight of our apparently unrewarded labors so oppressive in their density is on one side of the word. On the other rests an unchanging and unchangeable biblical truth

In 2 Timothy 1:12, Paul gives us a two-part anthem to follow his *nevertheless*. Either of the two is, by itself, wonderful. Together they are magnificent:

1. Paul says, "I know whom I have believed…" In the midst of trial by fire, who God is remains the greater, infinitely greater truth than what is happening. Plant your faith in the

miracles of God, and you are ripe for satanic attack. Anchor your soul in the God of miracles, and circumstances can never dislodge your hope. Whom you have believed may someday be all you have to cling to. The thing is, it will be enough.

2. "...and am persuaded that he is able to keep that which I have committed unto him against that day." Your life, faith and labors of love in Christ's behalf are not lost under the clutter of papers on God's disheveled desk. Regardless of what you may think just now, what you may actually hear Satan screaming in your ear, God keeps, carefully and lovingly, all that is committed into His hands. Nothing is lost. Nothing is even temporarily mislaid. In that day, that lovely dawn of clear bright truth, it will be right there where you put it, in His hands.

This part of the passage might well be translated top side down to read, "I know whom I have believed and am persuaded that he is able to keep that which he has committed unto me against that day."

Read that way it brings sweet assurance that God will not put any burden, any calling, responsibility or ministry in my hands that He will not keep in His. The ultimate responsibility for outcome is not mine—but His. My responsibility is to intentionally place back in His hands all that He puts in mine.

This is not just for the dying missionary, but for all who have felt unappreciated. The mom whose daily sacrifices are so carelessly trod upon by those for whom she labors. The steady-Freddy, the lusterless, unimaginative husband and father who pays the mortgage, hits the backyard grounders and attends the PTA. The retired executive who wonders if his former employees remember or appreciate his efforts to keep them all on the payroll through three recessions. The inner-city teacher who watches her dedicated creativity oozing its lifeblood on the floor of a dirty, gray classroom full of sneakered barbarians who care nothing about her heroic efforts to ignite some spark of life in them.

In the jeering din of demonic accusations of wastage, we can whisper the one great word that puts the enemy to flight and lights the corners of the room for all the unappreciated.

NEVERTHELESS

I know who my God is, and I am eternally convinced He will not let anything go unseen or unrewarded. When Satan tenderly drapes the dreary, but oh, so delicious afghan of self-pity around our slumping shoulders and begins to whisper, we need not let him even finish his sentence.

"What about all the…?"

Nevertheless.

"Who will repay all the…?"

Nevertheless.

"Look, they all forgot your…"

NEVERTHELESS

7

THE NEVERTHELESS OF
HOPE FOR THE LOST

Acts 17:34

The acid laughter of the intelligentsia rained down upon him like volcanic ash—hot, dry and deadly. How he had waited for this moment, prepared for it, not just since his conversion in Syria, but throughout his entire life. Few in his generation were as supremely educated as he was. Able to quote the great philosopher-poets in the classical Greek used by few except Areopogites, he had met the elite on their own ground and had precious little to show for it.

Behind him lay a life of radical faith and suffering. Ahead, the notoriously debauched citizenry of Corinth. But here, here in Athens, here before this renowned intellectual gallery on Mars Hill itself, Paul had hoped to access their souls through their minds, had expected to find identification with their culture and turn them to the Messiah. Instead, they laughed. Laughed! The stonings, beatings and imprisonments had not stung nearly so bitterly as the condescension of the brilliant.

Compared to Philippi, Ephesus and Thessalonica, and

later even Corinth, that cesspool of wickedness, the cool mockery Paul's brilliance earned him at Athens was an ironic defeat and failure. He left no church at Athens. He saw no revival, no mass conversions, no miracles, and he could not even manage to stir up a good riot. Nowhere in the New Testament is there a 1 or 2 Athenians. Nothing. Just a sigh of disappointment and determined resolve to preach Christ and Him crucified at Corinth, the next stop and one of the most perverted cities of that or any day.

Quietly, in the face of the unnerving futility of his longed-for evangelistic effort in Athens, Paul pronounces the one-word sentinel of hope: "Howbeit [Nevertheless] certain men…believed" (Acts 17:34).

Satan claims as his own slaves, insulated from any kingdom effort at rescue, entire populations whose deliverance seems not unlikely but impossible. Behind apparently impregnable walls of demonic deceit, tyrannical violence or intellectual pride (the worst of all), they languish in the grip of hell, and those who pray for their release long for some word of hope. Here it is.

Nevertheless, some believed.

There is no one anywhere in the world, in any circumstance of horror, utterly unreachable by the Spirit and the Word. A certain Hindu priest met Jesus in a dream, received a healing miracle for his wife and became an anointed Christian evangelist. The son of a Chinese communist party official, while working on his doctoral dissertation, had to look up certain biblical references that made no sense to him. The only Bible he was allowed to use was one kept in the pornography section of the local state-run library! Day after day, there amidst the filth, he found cleansing and salvation. Today, from the Philippines, he broadcasts the gospel in Chinese for the multiplied millions who wait in darkness.

In New York I met an elderly Jewish woman who met Christ alone in front of her television watching a man whose subsequent moral failure did absolutely nothing to make her doubt her salvation. She was a Holocaust survivor, surrounded by an impenetrable cultural wall, whose entire life and history and her every relationship made conversion to Christianity an utter impossibility. How could she hear? How could she ever believe?

NEVERTHELESS

This is great hope for all the waiting, praying, hurting Christians with loved ones busily building nightmares in the far country. You survey the crowd they run with, the atmosphere and the times, and despair like a fist pummels your faith. "Look," says the father of lies, "your daughter is a lesbian surrounded by lesbians who listen only to lesbians. How could she ever hear, let alone repent and come home?" Remember, she is no more unlikely a candidate than those who believed Paul's message on Mars Hill.

Dionysius and Damaris were real people, individuals

with real names, who were surrounded by the smug, deadening ether of intellectualism and stoic amorality. Despite all that, they believed. Why shouldn't your daughter? Remember, your child has something Dionysius and Damaris did not—*you* praying and saying the word of faith.

Nevertheless, some believed.

One million Americans languish in prison while you read this sentence. They are held behind walls of doubt, fear, violence, demonic evil, crushing insanity and a dehumanizing court system. But those walls cannot keep the Holy Spirit out. Many inside those walls will go on in lives of crime and corruption. Most, perhaps, will never escape the darkness and bondage that brought them down to the pit.

Nevertheless, some believed.

Is your loved one in prison? Why shouldn't he be the Dionysius of the state penitentiary? Why shouldn't your runaway be the Damaris of the streets who leaves the drugs and prostitution and comes home to you and your God?

Some shall believe. There is no reason in this world your loved one should not be among that "some." When Satan, or your own observant mind, paints for your emotions a picture of the pitiful bondage of your beloved, then own up to it. Yes, most in Athens rejected Christ. Most on Mars Hill laughed. Most, nearly all, turned their backs on Paul and his gospel. Nevertheless, Dionysius and Damaris believed. If them, then anyone.

Lord, do You see how they are living?

I AM God.

Of course, You are. Sorry, but their sin and unbelief are very frustrating to me.

Yes. I understand. Yours was to me.

Lord, I was never like that! Was I?

Just like that.

Well, they are going to be harder to reach than I was.

Nevertheless.

Lord, I am very discouraged here.

Nevertheless.

Lord, I....

Nevertheless.

Oh, I get it. That's what You want me to say.

Yikes!

Sorry, Lord. Nevertheless. Nevertheless. Like that?

Just like that.

In the bad old days when the Iron Curtain still hung across Europe, I sat next to two Czech college girls on a flight from Amsterdam to London. I read my Bible for awhile, unaware that one of them was watching. When I closed it, she reached over and traced the white cross on the cover with her fingertip.

She softly whispered a single word that I took to mean "cross." I repeated it the best I could, then pointed to my heart and said one word in English: "Christian." At that moment her companion reached across her and, seizing her wrist, began scolding her like a fishwife. After that the girl was quiet, avoiding my eyes all the way to London.

At the London airport as we gathered our belongings to deplane, the girl fumbled with her purse while her waspish traveling mate plunged up the aisle with Slavic ferocity. Certain that she was unobserved, she turned back to me and, placing her hand on her heart, repeated my single English word: "Christian."

The Soviets boasted that they had stamped out Christianity behind their iron veil. Satan gloated over a continent in spiritual blindness, and doubters concluded that the virtually corporeal darkness over Eastern Europe was impenetrable. Nevertheless, some—many, thousands—believed anyway. When the Iron Curtain fell we found them there, waiting patiently for outside Christians to arrive.

Is there someone or even a nation or a people group for whom you pray? Try this. Instead of saturation bombing, try a smart bomb. God knows who waits for salvation on the dark side of *nevertheless*. "Some believed." Concentrate your prayers of faith on that "some." If your son in prison has been resistant to the gospel, try praying for someone near him—his cellmate, an enemy or even a guard—to be touched.

Are you interceding for some unreached people group? Try this *nevertheless* prayer.

O God, You know who in this country or tribe is ready to believe. Satan has blinded the many. Nevertheless, some shall believe. Lord, concentrate Your Holy Spirit's power upon that "some," that the many might see and believe.

Are you discouraged by the apparent fruitlessness of your ministry? Only a few have believed? You are in good company. Paul left only a few believers in Athens. Pray this nevertheless prayer.

O God, my efforts are apparently without fruit. I confess to You that I am growing discouraged. Satan seems to have the upper hand. Nevertheless, some believed in Athens, and some shall believe here. Lead me to them, and them to me. Give me joy not in their numbers but in their names. Lord, if not all of Athens, then at least let me win Dionysius and Damaris.

Satan mocks such a prayer, but you have just the word to shut his mouth. Use it.

NEVERTHELESS

8

The Nevertheless of
Sin and Grace

Psalm 106

Catalogs of Israel's iniquitous rebellions are sprinkled across the pages of the Bible. None are more heartrending and forthright than the confession of unfaithfulness called Psalm 106.

Far from the contemporary generational blamesmanship, played so eagerly by modern America, the psalmist embraces a sincere corporate connectionalism that makes no distinction between the sins of the past and those of the present.

> We have sinned with our fathers,
> We have committed iniquity,
> We have done wickedly.
>
> —Psalm 106:6

Then comes a horrific laundry list of words of unrighteousness punctuated by God's acts of grace.

Our fathers understood not…they remembered not…thy mercies; but provoked him at…the Red sea.

—Psalm 106:7

NEVERTHELESS

He rebuked the Red sea…It was dried up…He led them through…He…redeemed them.

—Psalm 106:9–10

Then the sad saga begins again.

They soon forgot his works…
   They waited not for his counsel…
   They lusted exceedingly…
      They tested God in the desert…
      They envied Moses…
         They made a calf and worshiped it…
They changed their glory and became like beasts…
They forgot God, their Savior…
   They despised the pleasant land…
      They believed not his word…

They murmured…

They hearkened not to God…

They worshiped Baal…

They ate the sacrifices of the dead…

They provoked God to anger…

They angered him also…

They provoked Moses…

They did not destroy the nations as commanded…

They intermarried against God's will…

They learned the sins of the nations…

They served idols…

They sacrificed their sons and daughters unto demons…

They shed innocent blood…even their children's…

They polluted the land…

They were defiled…

They played the harlot…

They provoked God…

—PSALM 106:13–43, PARAPHRASED

NEVERTHELESS

He regarded their affliction when He heard their cry.

Twice in the first forty-four verses of Psalm 106, the nevertheless of divine grace surfaces gloriously in a sea of filth. The slime of sin, abomination and degradation ooze down across the face of this psalm. The psalm would be unbearable were it not for the two sightings of redemptive grace in verses 8 and 44.

"After all we've done," the psalmist writes, "even with all the nasty goop smeared on our faces, after all our faithless, fickle betrayals and backsliding, God still has a word to say. At the end of all the sins of the Hebrews in Exodus, comes the word."

> Nevertheless he saved them for his name's sake...
> —PSALM 106:8

Now find the boldness to peer into the toxic soup of our societal and personal horror. Pungent stuff. Harlotry, lust, idolatry, rebellion and child sacrifices whirl in the blender of human history until hopelessness and despair rise from it in noxious fumes. Then hear the word.

> Nevertheless he regarded their affliction, when he
> heard their cry: and he remembered for them his

covenant, and repented according to the multitude of his mercies. He made them also to be pitied of all those that carried them captives.

—PSALM 106:44–46

Perhaps the most hopeful and encouraging *nevertheless* in the entire Bible is that of His grace despite our sin. If God were blind or senile, His willingness to forgive and redeem us would not be nearly so wondrous. But God says He sees all, knows all, misses nothing, hates the sin we do and still, despite all that, finds within His divine character a nevertheless that reaches down to us in the muck and mire where we live.

Unfortunately, there is a counter nevertheless in Scripture as well. In fact, tragically, it is the most common usage of *nevertheless* in the Bible—by far!

It is the nevertheless of sin. God says, "Despite their sin, I forgive." In a vast multiplicity of texts, the goodness of God is celebrated in gloriously detailed lists, only to be followed by…

Nevertheless the children of Israel expelled not the Geshurites, nor the Maacathites [as they were commanded]…

—JOSHUA 13:13

Nevertheless the people refused to obey…

—1 SAMUEL 8:19

Nevertheless the high places were not taken
away; for the people offered and burnt incense
yet in the high places.

—1 KINGS 22:43

Nevertheless they departed not from the sins of
the house of Jeroboam…

—2 KINGS 13:6

Nevertheless the people did sacrifice still in the
high places…

—2 CHRONICLES 33:17

Nevertheless they were disobedient, and rebelled
against thee, and cast thy law behind their backs,
and slew thy prophets which testified against
them to turn them to thee, and they wrought
great provocations.

—NEHEMIAH 9:26

Nevertheless even him [Solomon] did
outlandish women cause to sin.

—NEHEMIAH 13:26

Nevertheless they did flatter him [God] with
their mouth, and they lied unto him with their
tongues.

—PSALM 78:36

Perhaps one monstrous, murderous example serves to

make the point best. In Matthew's Gospel, the fourteenth chapter, King Herod, inflamed with incestuous lust for his own niece, with whose mother, Herodias, he was already having an affair, promised the girl "with an oath" anything she wanted (Matt. 14:7).

What a pretty scene. Herodias virtually pimped her daughter to her brother-in-law with whom she was scandalizing the entire country. Evidently this woman's capacity for wanton wickedness was limitless. She prompted her daughter to ask for the head of John the Baptist on a platter.

The next line is a masterpiece (v. 9): "The king was sorry…"

That ranks right up there with, "I just want you to know this is not personal, but…" And right alongside, "I hope you don't think I take any satisfaction in this, but…" Or, "I hate to be the one to tell you this, but…"

Masterpieces! Brilliant strokes of rationalization. "The king was sorry…" He liked John the Baptist. He did not want to do murder. He felt beheading was extreme. He did not personally endorse the policy. Etc., etc., etc. Yada, yada, yada.

Then the clincher, "*Nevertheless* for the oath's sake, and them which sat with him at meat, he commanded it to be given her" (v. 9, emphasis added).

The nevertheless of sin is always preceded by some mealy-mouthed defense and followed by rationalization. "I personally disapprove of bar-hopping; nevertheless, these people are my friends." "Sure, this looks dangerous; nevertheless, it is also very exciting." "I know it's not exactly ethical and legal, and I hate that; nevertheless, everyone else is doing it, and if I don't, I may go out of business."

For Herod, the rationalization factor combined his oath, royal pride and the fear of others. He did not want to welch on a bet—at least, not in front of a room full of people. He was sorry. Sorry? I know that made John the Baptist feel better.

NEVERTHELESS

How very like our own is Herod's *nevertheless* and all this host of others from Psalm 106. Painful and sobering, this list is a sharp slap in the face, a stinging reminder that after the phrase, "I know this is wrong (a mistake) (sinful) (stupid) (insert your own word)"—that there is NO *nevertheless*.

Lord, we know You said to forgive one another; nevertheless...

You talk too much.

Too much, Lord?

You use too many words.

Which one should we leave out?

The last one.

We thought You liked that word.
Right word. Wrong sentence.
Yes, Lord, nevertheless.
What?
Sorry.

The good news is that after we have sullied any word, the Lord redeems it. We use *nevertheless* to rationalize our sin; God uses it to unleash His mercy and grace.

> If his children forsake my law, and walk not in my judgments; if they break my statutes, and keep not my commandments; then will I visit their transgression with the rod, and their iniquity with stripes.

NEVERTHELESS

> …my loving-kindness will I not utterly take from him, nor suffer my faithfulness to fail.
>
> —PSALM 89:30–33

> Nevertheless I will remember my covenant with thee in the days of thy youth, and I will establish unto thee an everlasting covenant.
>
> —EZEKIEL 16:60

They despised my judgments, and walked not in
my statues, but polluted my sabbaths: for their
heart went after their idols. Nevertheless mine
eye spared them from destroying them, neither
did I make an end of them.

—EZEKIEL 20:16-17

Psalm 106 pulls no punches concerning man's sin. It's
all there in plain language. But having cataloged our evil,
the psalmist reminds us of our hope. After all our
wickedness, after the sin is done and written down,
"Nevertheless he saved them" is so simply said and so
grandly done (v. 8).

Lord, we have sinned.

I have seen everything.

We feel so dirty.

You are dirty.

Don't You have anything better to say than that?

Yes.

What, Lord?

NEVERTHELESS

9

THE NEVERTHELESS OF THE SPIRIT

John 16:7, 13

John's chapter 16 begins rather like one of those terrible good news/bad news jokes. You know—the doctor tells the patient, "The bad news is your legs must be amputated. But the good news is the man in the next bed wants to buy your shoes."

Jesus says the bad news is that you will be put out of the synagogue, hated, even killed, and those who do these things to you will think they are serving God.

"What is the good news?" we can almost hear the apostles ask.

"Oh, the good news," the Lord answers. "I almost forgot that. The good news is, I'm leaving."

What? That's the good news? That cannot be the good part. We will endure hardship, go through the fire and be slaughtered like sheep, but not if You leave. That just can't be the good news.

NEVERTHELESS

Oh, *that* word. Please, Lord, it is wonderful how You use it. But this time, You have not followed it up very well. You list all these wretched things to befall us. OK, OK—we're there. We're ready to go through anything with You. Then You say, "*Nevertheless.*" We're still on the same page, Lord, but surely You mean something like…

Nevertheless, you won't really get hurt.

No, I don't mean that.

Or, nevertheless, like Job, you'll end up rich. That would be a good one. We like that one. How about that one?

No. Not that one.

What then, Lord? Surely You did not mean what You said.

Yes, I did. I always do. Nevertheless, it is expedient for you that I go away.

How can it be expedient for us that You go away, especially if all these bad things are about to happen to us? We can do anything, endure anything as long as we can see You and be with You. But, if You go away and all this evil befalls us, we may be weak.

You will see Me arrested, see Me crucified, dead and buried, and seeing Me will not make you strong. Your weakness and cowardice will be worse than you can now imagine. Seeing Me won't help.

Never, Lord, never! We will never betray you!

Trust Me. You will. Nevertheless, even that is not all bad. It will teach you how weak and fleshly you are. Such self-disillusionment will make you eager to receive the Spirit. That Spirit, not outside you, not extra-personal, but within you like breath, that Spirit is so needed, so powerful and empowering that it is, whether you can see it or not, good for you that I go away.

We disagree. Nothing could be better than You here with us.

Nevertheless.

You always say that.

It is not in spite of all we must endure, but precisely because of it, that Christ's physical departure from the earth was expedient for the church, for all of us who must live through all the rejections and deaths, deaths both great and small, that Jesus foretold in John 16:1–2. In fact, nothing, no other word in the entire New Testament, reveals the importance Jesus placed on our receiving and being filled with His Holy Spirit like…

NEVERTHELESS

The historical, physical Jesus, never limited in power, was profoundly limited by space and time. While in the body He could only be in one place at any given moment.

Yes, He was with the apostles in Jerusalem. Fine for them, but what about the Brits, who at that time were painting themselves blue and worshiping trees, or the Mayans who were practicing human sacrifice? A physical Jesus in Jerusalem means no Jesus at all in Mazatlan.

It was and is expedient for the whole lost world that Jesus go away and send His Holy Spirit. Wherever the Spirit-filled church is, Jesus is. The sun never sets on the body of Christ. The world needed first a savior. But with that work finished, Jesus knew that the world—the entire world all at once, not just Jerusalem or Bethlehem or Samaria or wherever He was at some precise moment— the whole world needed the Presence, the Body, the Touch, Word, Kerygma, Grace of Christ. That meant He must die, be planted in the ground like a seed, then be raised up as the multiplied body.

And there were certain Greeks among them that came up to worship at the feast: The same came therefore to Philip, which was of Bethsaida of Galilee, and desired him, saying, Sir, we would see Jesus. Philip cometh and telleth Andrew: and again Andrew and Philip tell Jesus. And Jesus answered them, saying, The hour is come, that the Son of man should be glorified. Verily, verily, I say unto you, Except a corn of wheat fall into the ground and die, it abideth alone: but if it die, it bringeth forth much fruit.

—JOHN 12:20–24

Surely in this passage the "fruit" is His Spirit-filled body, the church, ministering as He, in the body, could not do all over the world at the same time. Now, because of the Holy Spirit, there is no need for any Gentile, ever, anywhere to wait on the outside longing for a glimpse of Jesus.

More than geography is at issue here, however. The greater, more profound implication is in the words that immediately follow "Nevertheless." "*It is expedient for you.*" "You" means the apostles themselves, the immediate community of faith at the time of the crucifixion *and all believers for all time.*

Not for the doomed alone, but for the saved, it was expedient for Christ to go away and send the Holy Spirit. For two reasons: First, as with the lost, how many believers a day could He reprove, teach, comfort or encourage? How big a room, how great a temple could hold those believers who need His teaching or touch at any given moment?

Furthermore, and more importantly, Christ *with us,* even visibly, physically with us, cannot do all that His Spirit can do *in us.* So great is the internal ministry of the Holy Spirit, so magnificent His power, so munificent His gifting, so sanctifying His fire that it is expedient for us that the physical, extra-personal Christ return to heaven.

This means that the answer is grandly obvious to all those who ask, "Why should I pray to be filled with the Holy Spirit?" In short, because Jesus viewed it as so important that it was expedient for us that He Himself not be there for us to talk with and see and touch.

Lord, do not leave us. We plead with You. We cannot do it alone.

You shall not be alone.

Will You be here? Just as You are?

Yes.

You promise?

I already did.

But You said You're going away. How can You go away and be here at the same time?

Isn't that cool?

Lord, will the Holy Spirit teach us as You do?

Yes. Inside, He will talk to you inside.

What will He talk to us about?

Sin, for one thing.

Oh, that.

Yes, that and righteousness. And the judgment to come. I have many things I wanted to talk to you about, but you are not ready. Things so huge you cannot contain them,

but He will teach you.
We would rather You just said it all now.

NEVERTHELESS

Ah. That word again.
Nevertheless, when He, the Spirit of truth is come, He will guide you into all truth.

An inordinate fear that the believers will "hear a word" that is contrary to the Bible, or that arises from their own flesh or even from Satan, and act upon it keeps many today from hearing the Holy Spirit at all. There will always be charlatans and nitwits, but we dare not let them intimidate us into becoming spiritually deaf. The hyperspiritual nut cases who think they have the red phone to heaven do not invalidate Christ's promise that the Holy Spirit would be our teacher. The Holy Spirit hasn't gone anywhere, and He has not fallen mute.

On a flight out of Los Angeles recently the man next to me was delighted to discover that we were both ministers. He clouded over when he discovered that I, however, was ordained in a Pentecostal denomination. On the offensive in a split second, he began a provocative line of interrogation.

"Please," I begged, "let's not do this. I don't want a theological debate just now."

"No," he insisted, "just answer one question. Do you or do you not believe that since the close of the canon (the completion of the Bible) the Holy Spirit still speaks? We believe that the Scriptures are the full equipment for guidance and instruction. Do you believe people can still hear from God today?"

"All right," I sighed. "If you will answer my question, I will answer yours. You are a minister of the gospel. Were you called to preach, or did you take that office upon yourself?"

"I was called," he said.

"Who called you?" I asked.

His response was memorable. Nothing. Not a word. Nada. He just turned his face to the window and never spoke to me again. Ah, well, at least it was a peaceful trip.

I have things I want to say, but you cannot bear them now. Nevertheless…

But, Lord, can we trust this Holy Spirit?

He is the very Spirit of truth. Just as the Father told Me what to say, I will tell Him. He will never, ever tell you anything that is not from Me. He will glorify Me, quote Me and show you the things I want you to learn.

We would just so much rather sit at the table with You and ask questions.

Nevertheless, the Comforter will come.

But, Lord, we…

NEVERTHELESS

Yes, Lord, let Him come. We want to receive Him and hear Him.

Good idea.

10

THE NEVERTHELESS OF COMFORT AND COMMUNITY

2 Corinthians 7:6

There is a remarkable menagerie of words expressing pain of every kind in Paul's second letter to the church at Corinth—words like *affliction, anguish, beatings, distresses, fastings, fightings, labors, perils, persecutions, sorrows, stripes, sufferings, tears, tumults, weak* and *weakness*. They snap and snarl at the reader ferociously, in such obviously inconsolable anguish that comfort is unimaginable.

> When we were come into Macedonia, our flesh had no rest, but we were troubled on every side; without were fightings, within were fears.
>
> —2 CORINTHIANS 7:5

Yet even in the midst of the most pain-filled epistle in the New Testament, there is... *nevertheless*.

Nevertheless God, that comforteth those that are

cast down, comforted us by the coming of Titus;
and not by his coming only, but by the consolation
wherewith he was comforted in you, when he told
us your earnest desire, your mourning, your fervent
mind toward me; so that I rejoiced the more.

—2 CORINTHIANS 7:6–7

To be sure, the Holy Spirit is the Comforter, but Spirit-filled persons in community comfort one another. A friend having sent his little daughter up to bed heard her whimpering and went to check on her.

"What's the matter, darling?"

"Daddy, I'm scared in here alone."

"But you're not alone," he explained. "Jesus is right here with you."

"I know," she wailed. "But I want somebody with skin on his face."

We all do. The Scripture says that God inhabits the praises of His people. (See Psalm 22:3.) He also inhabits the comfort of His people. Beaten, afflicted, persecuted, suffering and weak, Paul the Apostle found the comfort of God—in Titus and in his report of the love and concern of the Christians at Corinth. Was it God who comforted Paul? Or was it Titus? The answer is "yes."

The community of faith does not scold the grieving widow for her grief or dismiss it lightly. The people of God dare not tell the hurting in their midst that they do not hurt, that they do not have a right to hurt. Even so, we are not wordless in the face of their pain. We do have one thing to say.

Nevertheless, we are here.

Like Titus, we are here. God in us, God as us can be with you and comfort you just as God comforted the great apostle through Titus.

Paul wrote in 2 Corinthians 7:6 that God "comforteth those that are cast down." If, as many seem to think, God is peevish with the downcast and irritated at their lack of faith, He would upbraid them, not comfort them. We the community of faith, like our God, must comfort the downcast who long for a word, a touch, a face with skin on it.

The nevertheless of Paul was a very human Titus. Likewise, for someone else, we are just on the other side of nevertheless from that person's deepest anguish.

John Wesley said, "I know of no holiness save social holiness." He meant that we do not live out our piety in relationship with God alone but in community with others. The downside of community is that no one can test your sanctification like your brother-in-law, the "antichrist." The upside is that just when you are ready to collapse under the unbearable weight of grief and suffering, Titus shows up with love letters from Corinth.

Some believers tend to so overspiritualize their faith that the relational aspect gets lost in the glow. Jesus painfully peeled away the soft spiritual goo to reveal the hard-core realities of relational holiness as no other teacher ever has. Probably that was a large part of what got Him killed.

The golden thematic thread that runs through the entire tapestry of the Sermon on the Mount is relational holiness. In that great teaching, theology (spiritual theory) was not Jesus' point. It was human application (spiritual practices). He was teaching, not about what we ought to believe, but about how we should act, love, live and forgive. If you want to get folks angry enough to kill you, just leave the theoretical realm and deal with horizontal, relational reality. Preach on love and win medals. Talk to a man about how he treats his mother-in-law and wind up nailed to the wall.

Jesus taught that everything—even, or perhaps especially, offerings to God—must be seen in the light of human relationships. "If thou bring thy gift to the altar, and there rememberest that thy brother hath aught against thee; leave there thy gift before the altar, and go thy way; first be reconciled to thy brother, and then come and offer thy gift" (Matt. 5:23–24).

The Bible never envisioned our being reconciled to God apart from our being reconciled to each other. No amount of spiritual language can change that. Indeed, another relational *nevertheless* in Ephesians beautifully bridges the gap between the spiritual and the pragmatic.

Paul offers a lovely expression of the truly spiritual and

mysterious relationship between Jesus and His bride, then quickly adds—"Nevertheless, this must be 'fleshed out' in decidedly flesh marriages." Paul saw that no human relationship can be separated from our relationship to God, even as our covenant with Christ can never be fully separated from our covenantal relationships on earth.

> This is a great mystery: but I speak concerning
> Christ and the church. Nevertheless let every one of
> you in particular so love his wife even as himself;
> and the wife see that she reverence her husband.
> —Ephesians 5:32–33

In chorus, husbands respond: Lord, we love you.

Love your wife also.

And wives chorus back: You see, Lord. You see how our husbands are. They are so unspiritual, so fleshly and…well…human. They do not understand how we enjoy praising You.

You must learn to enjoy praising them. Your husbands need your praise. They long for it.

And wives reply: That doesn't seem very spiritual, Lord.

Trust Me; it is.

And husbands echo: There, Lord. Now You see how they are.

I know how they are.
Of course You do, Lord. Then You know they are not all that easy to love sometimes.
And you? Are you always easy to love?
Now, in unison, husbands and wives cry out: Lord, make us spiritual. That is what we want.
Love and praise.
We are Your church. We love and praise You.
Love and praise each other also.
And wives chorus back: They are so hard to love and praise.
As husbands echo: We don't know how to love and praise them.

NEVERTHELESS

At last, husbands and wives respond: Yes, Lord.

11

The Nevertheless of the New Earth

2 Peter 3:13

When the crew of the *Enola Gay* dropped its single bomb on Hiroshima, they could not possibly have envisioned the devastation they were unleashing. Probably no one really did. Not even the great scientific and military masterminds back at White Sands could have known what would be the real ground-zero effect upon a city and the world of the newfangled bomb released from the *Enola Gay*.

Later, describing their emotions, that historic bomber crew spoke of an eerie silence that filled the plane as they circled back to survey the damage. Dumbstruck, awestruck, perhaps, they peered down at an entire city devastated by a single explosion, an explosion of unprecedented magnitude. The atomic bomb had arrived. Now we knew that we had the power to destroy the entire world.

Perhaps until that very moment certain biblical passages, though certainly to be taken on faith, passages that had seemed unbelievable, now hardly stretched the human imagination at all.

The day of the Lord will come as a thief in the night; in the which the heavens shall pass away with a great noise, and the elements shall melt with fervent heat, the earth also and the works that are therein shall be burned up.

—2 Peter 3:10

That is not to say that an atomic bomb or a hydrogen bomb or whatever hellish thing we can manage to invent next will actually be what is described in 2 Peter. It simply means that because man's monstrously fallen mind could invent an instrument of such horrific destructiveness as the atomic bomb turned out to be, we no longer had to stretch our credulity to envision what God could do.

Perhaps mere mortals could now set the sky on fire and dissolve the elements themselves. What chain reactions could we now set in motion to melt the molecular makeup of all we see? A firestorm of human invention might leap from neutron to neutron in a global conflagration that would burn water like oxygen and metal like wood.

The apostle Peter wrote of the "day of God, wherein the heavens being on fire shall be dissolved, and the elements shall melt with fervent heat" (2 Pet. 3:12).

Before the *Enola Gay* we could not imagine what that might look like. Now we can. And we tremble.

The last century was one hundred years of bloodshed. Two world wars and the mass murders by Stalin, Mao and

Hitler were certainly the centerpieces of the century's carnage, but they were, by no means, the end of it. Not even Alexander the Great or Genghis Khan or Nebuchadnezzar opened the river of blood that was the twentieth century. Caligula was an amateur compared to even our century's lesser mass murderers like Idi Amin and Pol Pot.

Not since the rise and fall of the Roman Empire has the world felt a social and geopolitical earthquake like the collapse of the Soviet Union. For seventy years the Russian Bear mangled captive Europe in its claws, only to hurl itself to the floor of human history in pathetic death throes and leave behind it civil war, racial cleansing and a continent in shambles.

Throughout the century, Africa, Central and South America and Southeast Asia remained, and yet remain, war torn in one country or another. In that painful century the United States floundered in Vietnam, savagery ripped Indonesia and slavery haunted the Sudan. Even today the persecution of the church in China continues to be a running sore that aches for a salve. The world is weary of crime, corruption and confusion. And there is no peace in Jerusalem.

With every new headline in the century we trembled. Economic uncertainty, world war, famine and AIDS were real products of the twentieth century. The United States and the West prided themselves on technology, conveniences and a "high standard of living," but murder in the streets, mayhem in the schools and a tidal wave of drugs were the horror behind the computer age. Child pornography, teen suicide and family disintegration either caused or came from mass alienation (who knows which). Alienation caused anger, anger became road rage, race rage and rage without a prefix. Wrath, like a noxious gas, seeped up from the city sewers to poison entire societies.

As if the twentieth century was not frightening enough, the twenty-first has risen with terror in its wings. In shock, the globe watched the worst single act of terrorism in history as the World Trade Center collapsed into rubble and thousands died. We asked ourselves two questions. What next? What is there to say?

The first question no one can answer, but we do know what to say.

NEVERTHELESS

Lord, we have ruined everything.

Yes, you have.

The sky is dirty, the rivers are poisoned, and we are corrupted.

Everything.

Everything. We confess.

Still…

Still what, Lord? Still what? Is there hope somewhere?
With Me there is.
Please, Lord, we have made this earth into a toxic dump. Please say something hopeful.
I have.
When, Lord? We missed it.
You forgot it.
Please, Lord. Please say it again.

NEVERTHELESS

Nevertheless…what?
Nevertheless, everything I ever promised.

When we have seen until our eyes are weary with seeing, one word, one great word, beckons us to look beyond the present age with all its nightmares and see what lies ahead. Despite all the filth and fevered sin that surround us there is still one great…

NEVERTHELESS

It breaks through this winter of our discontent and promises that despite what we see, the best is yet to come. When did we forget it? When did we, in the church, decide that the world was so good, that we were so good, that we could fix everything, heal everything, run everything on this earth so well that we no longer need the promise of a new one to come? When did we agree on that?

Regardless of what some may think or teach, the Scriptures are clear. This earth is not going to get better and better. It is going to get worse and worse. What scares the pants off of us about the twentieth century is that it has already yielded to the twenty-first, and there is no reason to expect it to be any better. But there is much logic behind expecting it to be worse.

Worse, not better, is the real history of the world. Things will not get better. They will get worse. Worse and worse and worse, and then they will get perfect and stay that way. That is the promise of Scripture.

After all we can do to pollute and corrupt each other, our world and ourselves, God remains undaunted and unchanged. We stare with despairing eyes at the nightmare of our making, and like shell-shocked children before a bombed-out house, we tell each other that nothing can ever make it right again. The sin and corruption are too great, the warring madness too violent and the drugs too ubiquitous for any of it to ever be right again. Comfortless orphans cannot comfort each other.

In this terrifying, wonderful moment the world may turn its infected eyes to the church and ask, "Don't *you* have anything to say to all this?"

We must respond with the great answer with which we ourselves have been gloriously answered.

NEVERTHELESS

Nevertheless we, according to his promise, look for new heavens and a new earth, wherein dwelleth righteousness.

—2 PETER 3:13

We survey the devastation of the World Trade Center like the dumbstruck crew of the *Enola Gay* and are astonished at the horror. Can there ever be righteousness, peace and beauty? We cannot imagine how.

NEVERTHELESS

If you enjoyed *Nevertheless*, here are some other titles from Charisma House that we think will minister to you...

The Missions Addiction
David Shibley
ISBN: 0-88419-772-7
Retail Price: $13.99

In these action-packed pages, you will discover a Global Jesus Generation that is creating discomfort in the church and change in missions worldwide. God is calling you to become part of a contagious epidemic of missions-hearted believers who will bring global fame to His name!

The Priestly Bride
Anna Rountree
ISBN: 0-88419-766-2
Retail Price: $13.99

The Priestly Bride contains a revelation that was given to the author and includes awesome insights into the processes of purification and sanctification that will take readers right to the heart of God. Within these pages is a spiritual quest into intense and dynamic levels of intimacy between the Bridegroom and His bride.

The Leading Edge
Jack Hayford
ISBN: 0-88419-757-3
Retail Price: $17.99

The Leading Edge contains twenty-four power-packed suggestions from Jack Hayford's best columns written for *Ministries Today,* with additional information and suggestions. Take an in-depth look at his leadership persona and identify rock-solid leadership skills that can help shape an individual into a great leader.

To pick up a copy of any of these titles, contact your local Christian bookstore or order online at www.charismawarehouse.com.